Tortured in America

The Life of a Targeted Individual

Michael Fleming

"Late last year, James Walbert went to court, to stop his former business associate from blasting him with mind-altering electromagnetic radiation. Walbert told the Sedgwick County, Kansas panel that Jeremiah Redford threatened him with "jolts of radiation" after a disagreement over a business deal. Later, Walbert, said, he began feeling electric shock sensations, hearing electronically generated tones, and getting popping and ringing sounds in his ears. On December 30th, the court decided in Walbert's favor, and issued a first-of-its-kind order of protection, banning Redford from using "electronic means" to further harass Walbert. No, seriously.

I recently took part in a BBC Radio 4 program, which took a light-hearted look into the "the real Manchurian Candidate" — and examined whether there is any truth in stories of mind control. It gave me a chance to talk about exotic non-lethal weapon concepts like the so-called telepathic raygun, the system which beams sound directly into your skull, and the "voice of god" talking fireball. Most of these projects are just lab experiments, or examples of Powerpoint engineering. But in some legal, policy, and business circles, electromagnetic brain assaults are being taken seriously.

Walbert's cause is supported by Jim Guest, a Republican member of the Missouri House of Representatives. He's working on proposed legislation to addresses electronic harassment, including a bill against the forced implantation of RFID chips. The U.N. is also now taking the possibility of electromagnetic terrorism against people seriously. And for the first time this year's European Symposium on Non-lethal Weapons included a session on the social implications of non-lethal weapons, with specific reference to "privacy-invasive remote interrogation and behavioral influence applications." Those who believe they are being targeted are getting a bit of official recognition.

For some, this opens up a new business opportunity. There are already quite a few companies out there offering "Technical Surveillance Counter Measures," or sweeps to determine if you are the victim of electronic harassment. As well detecting the usual bugging devices, they can check if you are being covertly bombarded by microwaves which may be the cause of "headache, eye irritation, dizziness, nausea, skin rash, facial swelling, weakness, fatigue, pain in joints and/or muscles, buzzing/ringing in ears."

Much of this trade may come from people with symptoms caused by something less exotic than high-tech military hardware. But companies will no doubt be willing to sell them expensive protection measures, anyway. And as awareness of these developing technology projects increases, we are likely to be hearing a lot more about "electronic harassment," "gang stalking" and the like over the next few years.

And there is also likely to be what folklorists call "Ostension," or acting out. Now that there are so many websites explaining how easy it is to harass people by zapping them with a modified microwave oven, sooner or later someone is bound to try it."

Article courtesy of Wired News.

Original source:
http://www.wired.com/2009/07/court-to-defendant-stop-blasting-t hat-mans-mind/

"If liberty means anything at all, it means the right to tell people what they do not want to hear.

The object of terrorism is terrorism. The object of oppression is oppression. The object of torture is torture. The object of murder is murder. The object of power is power. Now do you begin to understand me?"

-George Orwell, *1984*

Introduction

Numerous surveillance programs are performed on unsuspecting citizens. Although Americans knew that the NSA was spying on their phone calls, emails, and even some private homes — the Edward Snowden fiasco brought to our attention the vast reality of the NSA's spying program.

Did we need an official government document to prove what we already knew? Is reality only acceptable with a government document?

Years prior to the NSA "whistleblower" Edward Snowden, which released thousands of classified documents to the media, the NSA's "PRISM" program was listed in the Encyclopedia. In reality, the entire program was exposed before Edward Snowden stepped into the spotlight. Edward Snowden merely released documents that obtained proof of specific individuals and abuses that were used by the NSA's surveillance team.

A person becomes a "whistleblower" if they are a government employee, and speak out against wrongdoing within the government. A person becomes a "targeted individual" for much the same reason, but is not employed by the government.

Many federal laws exist to protect whistleblowers. For targeted individuals, otherwise known as "TIs" with a self-created label of injustice, mercy begins and ends with self-defense and local law enforcement agencies.

Becoming a targeted individual of our government is kept in secret. If you were to speak out against the government in countries such as North Korea, you would be tortured and/or killed in public. In America, this is done in secret.

There is no record of any nation that has not historically been involved in the targeting of its own citizens for exposing corruption. Every single government that has ever existed has multiple counts of human rights violations against activists.

Technological advances have allowed our government to torture citizens, silently (1).

COINTELPRO and Project Monarch: Disinformation Campaigns Against Whistleblowers

COINTELPRO was a program that was originally designed to silence government dissidents, end progressive anti-racism campaigns, and create paranoia and confusion between peaceful parties.

The KKK was infiltrated. The Black Panthers were infiltrated. If we ever wonder "who fired the first shot," there is no need to at this point. Agent Provacateurs, violence inciters, drama queens — are all around us.

Thousands of agents are employed by the FBI's Special Surveillance Group, the Joint Terrorism Task Force, and other extremely corrupt divisions in order to create the need for "national security." What I cannot begin to explain with words is known by every employee.

What I cannot understand for myself is performed by these agents on a daily basis. The FBI's SSG and JTTF's sole purpose is to create the need for security. How can you create a need for security? Quite simple, mi amigo. You create violence. Then, you foil your own plot. The villain is the criminal, yet also the good guy. Confusion is the key to creating violence. When everyone is confused, they lose their sense of security. When people lose their sense of security, they become afraid. When people become afraid, they defend themselves.

Quite simple human logic and nature at work. No "psychology" behind those who claim to be in the "intelligence" networks — yet sociopaths are <u>extremely</u> good liars and deceivers.

Better yet, guess what happens when a beautiful woman is employed as an agent?

Do we forget Neo in the Matrix? What happened when the "woman in the red dress" walked by Neo?

He got fooled.

I love women more than anything else in this world. Also, I am a man — and I know what they are capable of.
I'm not straying from the subject, but rather leading up to an important point.

If an individual were under surveillance by the government, by a beautiful woman, under the supposed protection of the (null and void) "Patriot Act," what if the local police found out? Would she be arrested for felony stalking? How many recruited "men" could she trick into harassing the TI by the end of the day?

With a smile and a slight wink — she could take over the block. The neighbors would hate the TI, the TI would only be left with two questions: "how and why?"

Now, we know how easy that it would be

to destroy someone's life. By creating a
supposed threat, by "men" wanting to please
any woman without question, based on their
own lustful desires for a woman that doesn't
give two shits about him (and thinks that
he's a total douchebag for even thinking of
participating in something so obviously
stupid and deceptive), the "conspiracy"
begins.

The "Occupy Protests" were labeled as a
"possible terrorist threat" by the FBI's
Joint Terrorism Task force.

It doesn't end there. It never does.

Incitement of violence was spread.
Plans to blow up bridges were shown to
members of Occupy by infiltrating agents.

What was once a peaceful protest,
became an angry mob. People were injured.
The NYPD shot a tear gas can into a woman's
face. People did not know who the terrorists
were, and everyone felt threatened. Not

because anyone there was a terrorist, but because the terrorists decided to show up and front as a protester. Does this ring a bell? Infiltration of the Black Panthers... same scenario.

Organizations such as "Greenpeace" were illegally raided after 9/11 by the FBI. Need I say more? I won't.

Disinformation campaigns. Please, please, do yourself a favor. Read about Operation Mockingbird if you ever, ever watch the news. This is past, present, and future. The media is the fourth branch of the government. Do not trust the media for your only source of information. Over half of the "terrorist plots" and "school shootings" were either performed by FBI informants (paid) or completely faked. Do yourself a favor, and do not believe whatever you see on TV. As with all channels, it's usually nothing more than a pathetic show that isn't worth watching.

Due Process and organized stalking. Where do we start with that subject? Due process is the only thing that separates the sophisticated from the classless. When illegal surveillance begins on a person, so does violence incitement. Never, ever believe anything that you hear about a person that claims targeting. Unfortunately, that person is a victim of control and filming. Nothing more, nothing less.

I also want to provide specific court cases that relate to forced implantation of RFID chips, as well as a court case regarding electronic harassment.

I do understand that some find this subject difficult to understand, and therefore, hard to believe. So, I will provide a "clear cut" court case for each instance — based on factual evidence that has been presented before a judge in a court of law: James Walberg. Please research the case and the transcript for more information. The original article, courtesy

of Wired News, is provided in the first few
pages of this book.

When COINTELPRO began in the 1960s, it
was known as the original form of "gang
stalking." This type of program was not new
to the American Government, however. This is
when it began to use it against its own
citizens.

In the early 1950s, the CIA paid a
group of "thugs and prostitutes" to destroy
a government. That government was about to
be replaced by a democracy, rather than the
current dictatorship. The CIA paid random
people to fight against and harass the
opposing forces, eventually sparking riots
that convinced the government to remain a
dictatorship (2).

Organized stalking proved to be an
effective measure in this situation,
especially considering that most of these
"thugs and prostitutes" were also drug users
— and therefore, would do anything for their

next "fix."

Project Monarch is the supposed "new name" for COINTELPRO. Project Monarch uses various surveillance methods to harass Targeted Individuals.

TIs experience 24/7 harassment, in an attempt to bring about one of the following:

1) *Suicide*
2) *A mental diagnosis (disinformation)*
3) *Homelessness / "Make them 'disappear'"*

Dr. Martin Luther King, one of the greatest (and most outspoken) men to ever walk the earth, was a COINTELPRO target for numerous years.

The FBI has been convicted in court of killing MLK Jr., but only in a civil case — similar to the murder of Nicole Simpson by OJ.

The easiest method to silence a dissenter, without drawing a guilty conscious (even for a sociopath without conscious who is afraid of prosecution), is the suicide of the target.

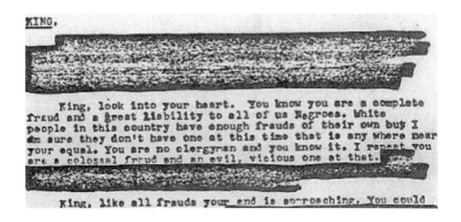

KING,

King, look into your heart. You know you are a complete fraud and a great liability to all of us Negroes. White people in this country have enough frauds of their own but I am sure they don't have one at this time that is any where near your equal. You are no clergyman and you know it. I repeat you are a colossal fraud and an evil, vicious one at that.

King, like all frauds your end is approaching. You could

It's obvious to everyone what happened — but it seems that justice just isn't served in some cases. With federal agencies — it is never served. After all, who prosecutes themselves for crimes committed?

"Dr. Martin Luther King's family and his personal friend and attorney, <u>William F. Pepper</u>, won a civil trial that found US government agencies guilty in the <u>wrongful</u>

death of Martin Luther King. _The 1999_
trial, _King Family versus Jowers and Other_
Unknown Co-Conspirators, is the only trial
ever conducted on the assassination of Dr.
King."

-The Martin Luther King Jr. Center.
Civil Case: King Family versus Jowers.
Transcript of closing statement

Disinformation, repression, and silence
are the keyword here. When a whistleblower
becomes a target, the ultimate goal is to
create the illusion that this person is
"insane."

I'll mention more about the suicide
goal in the last chapter with Ernest
Hemingway, who was driven insane by FBI
surveillance. Before Ernest Hemingway
committed suicide, and even ten years after
his death, many people believed that he was
insane. In fact, his own family believed
that he was "delusional."

After the FBI surveillance records were released, following Ernest Hemingway's suicide, it was a decade too late to believe what the writer was saying. One decade too late, one life cut too short.

Why? Was he a threat? A communist? No. He was Fidel Castro's "friend," which was otherwise known as someone whom he took a few photos with.

Cathy O'Brien is a very notable Project Monarch "participant" (victim). Cathy O'Brien stated that she had received constant harassment, surveillance, and other forms of "invisible" (electronic) torture.
Former FBI Chief Ted Gunderson also stated the same, after he had begun to perform speeches about various forms of corruption within the FBI.

Enough examples. Let's explore some "no-name" TIs. The "unimportant" ones who are buried by dozens of hired felony stalkers.

Most of the programs that whistleblowers expose are related to government corruption that ultimately results in the death of multiple individuals. Such examples are "false-flag" war operations, cloud seeding experiments, and illegal government tests.

Tis are not "tattletales," or anarchists. Tis, in most circumstances, are peace activists and inventors. The more outspoken that a TI is, the more creative that they become, the less of a slave that they are. We must first realize that we are a slave before we know that we have to become free.

The government has a multitide of individuals to make sure that this never happens. Progression is change, and change threatens stability. Not the stability of the country, the economy, or national security. Change threatens their job. Peace threatens war. War cessation threatens their paycheck.

I know how governments work. I dated a
Department of Defense secretary who
"inflates the budget on purpose" to
"increase the Department of Defense's
funding." I knew another person who was
contracted for the Department of Defense,
who gave me the same exact answer.

"They said, 'we can increase the budget
next year, but we have to spend
such-and-such amount this year. Find how
much that we have to spend, make it fit into
someone's paycheck, and get us the
increase.' And I paid a guy $40 per hour to
enter Excel spreadsheets. It's normally $10
per hour work.'"

For some reason, I wasn't surprised
when I heard this. I'm sure that none of us
are. We all know what really goes on, but
denial sometimes gets the best of us. Truth
is extremely difficult to fathom; simply
because it is stranger than fiction.

Instances such as these, when the government is threatened to answer for what they do or risks losing a taxpayer-funded paycheck, a retaliation is applied.

As a Ponsi scheme artist runs from the truth while embezzling more people's money along the way, the Ponsi scheme artist must feel that he is in control of the situation at all times.

Much as a man beats his wife and mentally abuses her to feel — how shall I say — just bad enough to keep from leaving him. If the woman thinks that she doesn't deserve better, just like the control-freak tells her, she won't leave him to see that she does deserve better. Much, much better. At the time, she just doesn't know it. Like a taskmaster whips a slave into submission, a TI is beaten into the dust from which they came.

If a whistleblower or TI is simply

killed, the disinformation campaign does not work as well (obviously).

After all, everyone has perception. Wouldn't the general public eventually "figure it out" if every whistleblower or targeted individual started dying from "natural causes?"

Disinformation campaigns are the ultimate choice for any government "security" agency. Targeting the individual's sense of reality is the only way to disprove what has been done by the government. After all, can the TI prove what he or she says? More than likely, yes. However, who would believe that such a huge conspiracy exists against an "unimportant" person?

In the eyes of a stalker, the unimportant person is nothing more than a dog to beat. The child that stands over the animal, feeling powerful because the animal is under their control. Abusers love power.

What they love more is money — and for
performing felony stalking under the
umbrella of "national security" - what more
could a creep ask for?

The government is guilty of a huge
crime, which is punishable by life
imprisonment (most whistleblower-exposed
crimes involve acts of treason). The only
thing left to do, is to make the general
public think that this individual is nuts,
so that they do not believe what is being
said by that individual.

This is the equivalent of the Nazis
versus the Jews in the 1940s. The Nazis
always spread lies and rumors, stating that
"Jews were the problem in society."

In those days, Jews were the doctors,
the lawyers — the white-collared geniuses.
Not anymore, under Hitler's watch.

So now that we know these programs
actually exist, and have for quite some

time, we will explore what happens to these "whistleblowers," and TIs that decide to expose illegal and immoral programs within our government.

Organized "Gang" Stalking and Electronic Harassment

Although electronic weapons (also known as "directed energy weapons") have been around for quite some time, most of the general public is still oblivious to their existence.

Directed energy weapons are a rather simple method of harassment, and are only illegal in one state currently — which is Michigan (*Act* No. 256. Public Acts of 2003).

"Gang stalkers" use directed energy weapons, some as simple as a cell phone, to torture and manipulate whistleblowers into a state of silence. There is also significant circumstantial evidence that "Gwen towers" are used to target specific individuals, and that topic is covered in great detail within Jesse Ventura's Tru-TV Network "Conspiracy Theory" episode "Brain Invaders."

Methods of intimidation intend to

silence government dissidents through remote control — which furthers the anger of the targeted individual — as he or she is unable to defend themselves against electronic weapons.

Noise campaigns against the individual are incessant. Whether it is by "Voice of God" technology or by actual neighborhood disruption (i.e. horn honking, loud after-market mufflers, personal harassment via "sniffling" or other annoyances), the noise campaign is almost immediately implemented as a first goal for the affected.

As with Pavlov experiments performed with dogs and other animals: the target can be placed under surveillance and "measured" to see their reaction to each individual sound. From that point on, it is used as an incitement and attention-seeking technique. The goal of stalking is to keep the focus on the stalkers. The objective for the affected is to "not feed the trolls." Feeding a troll is like feeding a stray dog. They will only come around for more food.

The individual feels helpless, and relies on police to stop what everyone seems to know is going on.

If the individual reacts to the stalking and harassment with physical violence, the TI will be the one who appears to be the problem in society.

This is <u>exactly</u> the goal and the point of electronic harassment.

Methods that are used against targeted individuals include:

1) *"Voice of God weapons"*
2) *Active Denial Systems*
3) *Mind Control via RFID*
4) *Constant Stalking*
5) *Aerosol Targeting*

"Voice of God" weapons are otherwise

known as "Directed Radio Frequency" signals.

Directed radio frequencies can penetrate the individual's mind, causing them to hear voices or sounds that nobody else can hear. Unlike a mental illness, this is not a hallucination. The human brain operates on a certain frequency, and with the simple knowledge of that frequency, the human mind can be easily manipulated.

In the case of Patent 5159703, the frequency is directed into the individual's skull through radio frequencies, similar to a radio receiving a music or voice transmission. In this instance, however, only the person that is meant to receive the transmission will hear the "radio" transmission. This is done rather simply and easily — yet the "intelligence" agents think that it is somehow ingenious.

By funneling an antenna into a laser-directed beam, only the receiving point will hear the radio frequency. Very simple. Two men with two tin cans and a string, yet one man is not holding the other end — and the "man" at the other end of the tin can is actually one of the lowest forms of life that you could ever imagine... a stalker.

A great video to watch on this subject is Jesse Ventura's Conspiracy Theory Episode, "Brain Invaders." This episode completely describes the torture that these individuals go through on a daily basis due to VOG weapons.

Active Denial Systems are easily obtainable, and are a prime weapon in "gang stalking." ADS uses an ultra-high microwave frequency to "cook" the individual's flesh, penetrating a few millimeters through the skin — creating a very uncomfortable heat sensation that tends to annoy the targeted individual. With the use of a simple light or invisible radio-emission tool, the target is able to be harassed — especially during their sleep.

Mind control is a rather easy subject to touch on, although most people don't even know that such a technology even exists.

Mind control has been researched by the CIA since the 1950s, and the research has allowed mind control to be performed wirelessly — without the individual's knowledge.

Unlike MK-Ultra, the victim has no idea that they are under mind control. This is much similar to hypnosis — causing the person to do something without their consent or freewill to choose. With RFID technology, mind-control has become one of the simplest tactics to implement on a TI. Although the individual may or may not remember the experience that took place under mind control, the individual knows that it wasn't themselves that performed those actions.

Government "patsies" are excellent examples of this; who have long been used to fulfill government assassinations and other extreme plots of terror.

One minute, the guy is shooting someone. The next, he is reading "Catcher in the Rye," waiting on police to escort him to his prison cell.

May I also make a note of interest about John Lennon's assassination... John Lennon, and his wife Yoko Ono, were both targets of COINTELPRO.

President Hoover wanted to have both individuals "deported" - especially after producing the hit song "Give Peace a Chance." Shortly afterwards, a huge nationwide anti-Beatles campaign began, and hundreds of people burned their Beatles memorabilia.

Need I say more?

Back to RFID. RFID implementation and individualization is rather easy, actually.

All that is required is one person, one 0.4mm RFID chip, and a parked vehicle. In more sophisticated instances, large tracking devices are covertly installed on vehicles, usually under the hood or wheel wells [4].

The unsuspecting TI will exit from the store on their daily routine, and feel a small sting — usually in their back. Using various "injection methods" from a distance, the target will go to work, school, home, or anywhere outside — the target can become easily "chipped" without their knowledge.

Blow darts were used during the era of Japanese ninjas, and are even featured in popular video games such as "Assassin's Creed."

For assassination techniques, a closer technique is used. For anti-fluff purposes in my writings, I will not detail into this subject — but further readings and videos are available online by searching the term "umbrella assassin."

RFID, short for "Radio Frequency Identification," is a very sophisticated, yet so simple, method of torture and harassment.

Unfortunately, RFID materials have been consumed by every living being on the planet. RFID ink, RFID chips, and RFID tags are all around us — all day long.

How does Wal-Mart know when a thief snatches a CD player? The RFID tag. How does the mechanic know that you haven't had a tune-up in a year? The RFID tag. How can you tap your credit card against a reader and give your information to a sensor? An RFID tag.

Everything is "tagged," and so is "everyone." Further information will be explained in the "aerosol targeting" portion of this writing.

Each RFID chip is programmed to a

specific number, a specific frequency. These same RFID chips are now used to track pets and children via satellite.

Passive RFID chips (non-self powered) gain operation through passing wireless Internet waves, cell phone towers, and other wireless electronic equipment. Losing a signal on RFID ink or an RFID chip is nearly impossible with the Verizon "can you hear me now" coverage map.

"Winston says that Oceania's world of telescreens and Thought Police means that there are 'always the eyes watching you and the voice enveloping you. Asleep or awake, working or eating, indoors or out of doors, in the bath or in bed—no escape.'"

Although I make many references to the 1984 George Orwell film, I must reiterate the cult following of the once science-fiction classic. There are people who want this for society. There are control freaks. There are millions of sociopaths. There are serial killers free, roaming the streets, as we speak.

Surveillance has not stopped any of them. Nothing, nada, zip — zilch.

I am not against surveillance in public. I believe that if a person chooses to enter downtown Las Vegas, on the strip, and gets shot by someone else — as has happened multiple times — we need some proof in court as to who performed the shooting. Who would not agree? Why would a camera not be pointed at a location that is known for violence?

Once a man steps foot inside of his home, once a man pulls into his parking lot, what he does inside of his home is strictly his business. When a man calls his wife to ask what she would like for dinner, the NSA has no business knowing about their chicken soup while "preventing terrorism."

This is rather obvious for most of us.

I do believe that some good people exist within the NSA, FBI, and CIA. I believe that they are also kept quiet, just as Tis are kept quiet.

People who know too much also know that if they speak too much — they will be silenced.

One of the main goals of the disinformation campaign via stalking and harassment, as stated, is to silence the individual. Cause a provocation. Violence. Create a hermit, a recluse, a "paranoid."

Stalking will cause an individual to become violent, aggressive, and withdrawn. The targeted individual that experiences stalking, like anyone else who has experienced the worst crime known to date, will wish for retaliation against their perpetrators. However, they continue to experience the same stalking, day after day.

Stalking is the equivalent of rape.

When a man rapes a woman, he forces himself into her personal space. Her protected, personal, private space.

People who stalk people and rape people, unfortunately, have no hope in life. They have committed, in my mind, an unforgivable crime.

I would take a bullet for any of my fellow men. I would watch a rapist die in the electric chair without personal conviction. I have no sympathy for the only crime against God-given freewill — which is stealing

someone else's freewill of choice from them.

Of course the self-defense method is out against stalkers. How can you defend against someone who stalks you on a public street?

The individual may contact the police, may ask family or friends for help — only to

portray themselves as a delusional "victim."
When a targeted individual tells police that
they have multiple stalkers, and explains
that they are stalked by an organization
such as the CIA, FBI, or NSA - the
individual is automatically labeled as
insane. That is, unless the police officer
knows the true history of these
organizations.

The reality of the CIA, the FBI, the
NSA is not very difficult to grasp. All of
these organizations claim to "watch"
individuals. All three organizations are spy
organizations, and to ever think that these
individuals are nothing more than stalkers
with badges — would be rather ignorant.
However, some people in society actually
believe that these organizations are
"important." They "protect us from
terrorism." The irony of that statement
could never be more entertaining.

Aerosol targeting can be used to
improve the disinformation campaign, and

rather quickly. Within geoengineering, aerosol particles are released with a positive charge (i.e. NASA's "CARE" program, short for Charged Aerosol Release Experiment).

Example materials include:

1) *Manganese Sulfate*

2) *Iron Sulfate*

3) *Barium Sulfate*

4) *Gram-negative Soil Bacteria — i.e. Morgellons (Wikipedia, Bioprecipitation)*

5) *Aluminum*

These materials can cause the individual to seem autistic, dyslexic, disorientated, and over-emotional.

Targeting the individual is rather easy, actually, because all that someone would have to do is create a negative charge within the individual's home. In physics, we all know that "opposites attract." Electricity must flow from a positive to a

negative pole in order to produce a flow.
Otherwise, it is a dead charge.

Directed negative ion generators can be
pointed at the target's window, which
"attracts" the positive particles. Raytheon
has created multiple weapons that are now
used against American citizens, such as
Radio Frequency emission devices — which are
used to target homes and individuals within
the homes.

While the individual smells sulfur and
aluminum, their neighbors seem to be fine.
Actually, the neighbors seem to think that
the targeted individual is "going crazy." An
overload of these particles can cause severe
problems for the targeted individual;
emotionally, mentally, and physically.

Although everyone (obviously) is
affected by the aerosol releases, the
individual who is targeted will seem the
most affected. It is similar to dumbing down
the Nazis with meth, while fluoridating the

Jews' water supply to keep them complacent. Both the Nazis and the Jews, in this case, are made to be "mindless drones."

If an individual is excessively outspoken, he or she can be targeted by individual aircraft.

The aircraft, usually using bogus names and missions such as "JIA" Cessna aircraft or passenger-less American Eagle aircraft, can be used to "distribute" materials over the target's home. Evergreen Aviation, located at Pinal Air Park in Marana, Arizona, is a CIA base that is used to store hundreds of passenger aircraft — that are not used to transport passengers. Once labeled a "bone-yard," which is nothing more than a present-day aircraft chop shop.

This is the easiest way to cause a target to appear insane. After all, who would believe them — if they tried to tell someone that the "CIA was attacking them with planes?" Although the aircraft has no

purpose in the sky, although they are
emitting visible chemicals from their bow
(and are even registered to Pinal Air Park
in some cases), who would believe that these
planes are actually committing acts of
treason on American citizens?

   Most people would rather believe
whatever Glenn Beck says, to be honest.
Nothing personal against Glenn Beck, but —
if you're perceptive — you can easily get my
point from that statement.

   "History is a set of lies agreed upon."

   *-Napoleon Bonaparte, (Orchestrated a
   holocaust with sulfur dioxide)*

RFID Technology: Unlimited Potential, Inescapable Torment

RFID technology has long been researched, as early as the 1950s — and began official implementation back in the 1980s. RFID programs were originally used to research GPS tracking and defense systems — and have now begun to be used as identification and weapon technology.

RFID is able to completely "control" an individual, based on a simple frequency that can influence the individual's mind beyond the point of self-control.

In the 1960s, a bull was used as a "mind-control test" experiment. The bull was programmed to a certain "frequency" after being implanted with an RFID chip. The bull was "told" to attack, then told to "calm down." The experiment drew much attention by military intelligence, because it worked (3).

With a simple wireless frequency, a
bull stopped in mid-stride, refusing to
attack the red sheet that he once knew as a
threat. The bull immediately changed his
character with one simple frequency, and
decided that red carpets weren't that bad
after all.

Why was this research performed by the
CIA? For bulls to not attack red carpets?
No. This research was performed on bulls, in
order to be perfected — for humans.

Human mind control, notably that of the
MK-Ultra program, involved giving
"unsuspecting individuals" large amounts of
LSD. A great example of what happens to
people who participate in this program
include: Ted Kaczynski — the Unabomber.

The Unabomber was a participant in the
MK-Ultra program.

Once a Harvard genius, now a criminal,
the Unabomber confessed multiple times that

it was not his fault that he performed these actions. Nobody believed him.

However, official government documents state that he received multiple doses of LSD during the MK-Ultra research. Why was this not included in the criminal case against him?

The answer is simple. Government patsies are meant to look "insane." They aren't meant to ever be believed for telling the truth.

When the Roman Empire wanted Jesus to die, they accused him of treason. When they could not get the general population to agree to his death, they decided to figure out a way to make the population hate him.

By provoking the accused, by creating a violent manifesto of confusion, as was seen by Jesus turning over the tables within the temple (shortly after the planning by the Roman Empire), the general population cheered his death.

An innocent man still, even after the
fact — yet what seemed to be violence
stirred by the man who called himself God —
was an example to those of us who lived
after him.

Innocence is sniffed out like a rabid
dog finds rotten flesh. No good deed goes
unpunished. This excludes no-one. Always
remember who owns this world, and never
forget who put us here.

If a government will kill Jesus for
speaking the truth, if a government will
exile Moses for asking to free slaves, if a
government will fight a war over keeping
slaves so that they do not have to work the
fields themselves — imagine what they will
do for a paycheck.

Culture has changed, humanity has not.

For us "decent people," most of these

ideas seem insane. Absurd. Can't happen.
Right?

Why?

We see through our own filter. We have
a filter installed on our eyes, which is our
personality. A naive person can be trusted,
99% of the time. Naive people do not see
what is heading towards them... because they
never create the train that would head down
someone else's track.

In my personal experience, after
20-some odd years of being naïve myself, I
have learned to trust no-one.

I forgive, I forget. I hold no grudges,
and I still cannot fathom how others do. I
live in the present, I hope for the future.
Some rail on the past.

Regardless, you must learn from the
past — while not living inside of it. If we
know that organizations are corrupt, we know

that they are likely to commit the same crimes in the future. If reforms are not present in someone's life after past mistakes, neither will they be for corrupt organizations.

The NSA and the FBI spied on MLK Jr., as mentioned.

There is no communist threat. There is no terrorist threat. There is a real threat. There is the threat to our personal liberty.

There are two sides to a coin, and there are only two types of people. When I was a salesman, I learned a phrase called "KISS." It was short for "Keep It Simple, Stupid." I reminded myself of it often during my sales pitches.

What does it mean? How does it apply in life?

There are two poles to energy. Two sides to everything. As Morgan Freeman

states: "there are two types of people...
good people, and bad people."

There is simply no other way to clarify
what we face on a daily basis.

The Ultimate Goal of Government Surveillance: A Repeat of Ernest Hemingway's Life

For many years after the death of Ernest Hemingway, most of his friends and family thought that he had simply "went nuts" and shot himself.

Ernest Hemingway, believing federal agents were pursuing him, said "It's the worst hell. The goddamnest hell. They've bugged everything. That's why we're using Duke's car. Mine's bugged. Everything's bugged. Can't use the phone. Mail intercepted. What put me on to it was that phone call with you. You remember we got disconnected? That tipped their hand."

In 1999 Hotchner reported that through the Freedom of Information Act, he had discovered that the FBI and J. Edgar Hoover had, in fact, bugged Ernest Hemingway's telephone.

The single most important part of this entire book, the entire point of the story, is that so many people are labeled "delusional" for thinking that the CIA or the FBI is "out to get them."

Actually, this statement is labeled as a symptom of schizophrenia or psychosis in the DSM. However, I must state again, what do these organizations do for a living? They spy on people.

Some who claim stalking instances are delusional, obviously. Usually, its the same people who see pink fairies or purple zebras in their backyard. I'm not talking about those people.

I'm talking about the number one crime in America, considering all crimes committed: stalking. Stalking is, however, the crime that is ignored and unjustified more than any other crime — yet is more frustrating for the victim than could ever be imagined.

No boy cries wolf unless he:

1) Sees a wolf.

2) Wants attention.

3) -or- is insane.

There is one of the three attached to each individual who claims to be a TI. It is up to police and investigators to find out which. All claims of stalking should be investigated thoroughly, as it is an extremely difficult matter for the truly targeted to deal with.

I will offer a recommendation for targeted individuals. I recommend that you contact police when you notice multiple instances of the same thing. Do not give police details of what is going on. Remember what I mentioned in the previous chapter? Leave the investigating to the investigators. (KISS, Keep It Simple, Stupid.)

Report facts (only) to the police. Let the police do their job and investigate the rest of the case for you. Never assume anything, always do something different and out of sorts.

Routines and schedules, for a stalker, are like a daily agenda for them to plan out for your life.

If you go to work at 9am, the agenda for your stalker could include your home being broken into by 10am. If you call into work that day, you just ruined the stalkers plan. In cases of "gang stalking" or organized stalking, communication is required. Meet-ups are usual, telecommunications are rare, texts are frequent.

As the FBI loves to involve the community in their harassment campaign against citizens, which accomplishes multiple goals at the same time (trains the public to hate and distrust while recruiting

free workers), you can always remember that
police and the NSA have some people under
strict surveillance — and it has nothing to
do with your instance of stalking.

Let them get a cokehead to stalk you.
Let the cokehead run around your block 20
times, until he runs out of cocaine. What
will he do? Text someone for more cocaine.
The police are already watching him —
because crackheads are just pretty obvious
to police and the neighborhood in general.

So, when a cokehead becomes an
"informant" - which is already under
legitimate surveillance by police — guess
what else that the police find out?

That you are being stalked and harassed
by the cokehead/crackhead. This draws
attention, clarifies the situation, and
relieves you of all accusations of
"paranoia" and/or delusion.

Be thankful when they hire a crackhead

as an "informant." It's your leprechaun that
points to the pot of gold under your
rainbow.

I question the fact that people who are
truly under surveillance are ever labeled as
"delusional or paranoid."

Official government documents prove
that Ernest Hemingway, a classic American
author, was under surveillance for nearly 20
years — without cause. It ultimately led to
his death, and J. Edgar Hoover and the FBI
is responsible for his torture and murder.

Jean Seberg, God rest her soul, was a
beautiful, talented, and successful actress.
One day, President Hoover and the FBI
decided to take interest in her.

What did Jean Seberg do? Did she commit
a crime?

Jean Seberg contributed to the Black
Panther party during the civil rights

movement. She gave approximately $10,500 in cash and gifts to the organization.

President Hoover released authorization to the FBI to "neutralize her."

What this meant to COINTELPRO agents — was to have her killed. What followed was not a murder by gun, by knife, by any weapon — other than the most deadly weapon known to man: stress.

A smear campaign was formed against Jean Seberg. Rumors were spread that "she was pregnant with a Black Panther's baby."

The campaign against Seberg began. Her baby was born as a stillborn, according to her doctor, from stress. She began to move from place to place, seeking peace and asylum. She committed suicide. She was "neutralized."

This is one example of many, and the ultimate goal of organized stalking and surveillance. While the criminals roam free, people who work for a living are stalked, harassed, and tortured — for no reason.

These people, presently numbering in the thousands, report the same detailed explanations of something that they are not able to stop. Former CIA officials and "Voice of God" weapons creators verify the existence of these programs.

Stalking, with harassment, is a felony.

Why does this continue? Is America seeking the fourth reich, the next holocaust? Isn't this exactly what Hitler did prior to World War II?

Honestly, I wouldn't expect much more from the current administration — and from the previous.

George W. Bush and Barack H. Obama are the same to me as Hoover and Nixon. Lying scam artists. Nothing more, nothing less.

Communism? Terrorism? What group is next? The boogeymen are always after America.

The surveillance state will always save us from the invisible presence that threatens our existence by destroying our lives — and watching over us like our own personal guardian demon, or the fox watching the henhouse.

Never trust a stalker. Period.

The Charles Manson Cult: Teachers of Harassment to Project Monarch

The Charles Manson Cult was notably one of the sickest and most demented cults in American history.

Charles Manson and his cult members would break into homes of good people, such as policemen and well-known actors, and would rearrange items within the home to "freak them out." When the actors and policemen would arrive home, they would find things rearranged — and would instantly question their own sanity. After this happened to them multiple times, they knew that something was up. Some died with the words "PIG" written on the wall.

I name the Jeffery R. MacDonald case, where a man was convicted of killing his entire family and blaming it on cult members. Was MacDonald guilty? Only God knows.

However, I know this fact... MacDonald was not guilty beyond a reasonable doubt. The evidence submitted in court behind his case, which resulted in a life sentence, was completely flawed and tainted. Not only this — but MacDonald was investigating a serious accusation at a military base during the murder. Jeffery MacDonald was looking into accusations that the CIA had imported drugs through American soldiers' body cavities that had returned from Vietnam. The bodies were emptied of drugs, then prepped for funeral. The drugs were sold on the street at street value — and a war of millions turned into profit of billions for the Central Intelligence Agency.

Although the fact was verified by other persons, MacDonald was one of the original lead investigators into the case. If anyone had motive against his family and himself, guess who it would've been? Not MacDonald himself.

Nevertheless, I do not dabble in

conspiracy theories. If I spew a theory in a factual book — I will always state the word "theory." I pick my battles, and I am careful to only state facts where evidence can be provided. As for MacDonald, as I previously stated, only God, MacDonald, and his family know exactly what happened that day.

I'm straying from the subject, but you can easily see my point from that example.

When you mess with the government, no good deed goes unpunished. The Unabomber is also serving a life sentence, as mentioned, for a succeeded MK-Ultra test by the Central Intelligence Agency.

Back to Manson.

Charles Manson and his minions would hide out inside of the actors' homes, and watch their reaction to the furniture rearrangements. He and his cult group seemed to somehow enjoy freaking people out. With

Project Monarch, we have thousands of
reports of the same exact situation.

As always, two independent witnesses is
enough to convict anyone in court. However,
nothing seems to be done about Project
Monarch — the new COINTELPRO.

Why?

If Americans understood who is taking
over their country, they would do something
about it. Not until people start dying,
people begin to see themselves threatened
personally, will anything ever happen. The
reality is — we are all in the same melting
pot. We are all affected by this disgusting
and disturbing behavior that is allowed to
exist.

The only hope that we have to change
this is not the destruction of these
organizations — as many would seem to think.

There are good people within the FBI,

the CIA, and the NSA. Good people who are deceived into doing bad things, that is. We must remember, some people actually believe that we are under a terrorist threat. Some people actually believe that suicide bombers are any different from George W. Bush, who also bombed innocent people without cause.

Those people are our only lifeline. They are the only ones left who are able to change our situation. Those within the organizations that are corrupt, who refuse to also be corrupt themselves, will find themselves in an odd situation. Like the puzzle piece that just doesn't fit, that belongs in another puzzle, so to speak.

So, what will it take to end this madness? Should electronic equipment be shut down, so that abusers of the system will not have access to it?

In my opinion, laws should be put in place to stop this disgusting and cruel act of torture against our own citizens.

People who believe that 9/11 was an "inside job" are not terrorists, they are called "smart and logical." People who speak out against cloud seeding are not "anti-patriotic," they are merely trying to save their own citizens from the next cloud-seeded tornado or rainstorm.

Whistleblowers experience this type of torture daily. Why does nobody care? The whistleblowers tell you the truth so that you are able to make an informed decision from it. When whistleblowers expose the truth, they are not being "tattletales" or haters of the government.

Whistleblowers simply give a shit about other people. That's it. Whistleblowers give a shit enough about other people to save them; even if it means risking their own life.

"...but it's also interesting to notice who it is we assassinate. D'you ever notice who it is... stop to think who it is we kill? It's always people who've told us to to live together in harmony and try to love one another.

Jesus, Gandhi, Lincoln, John Kennedy, Bobby Kennedy, Martin Luther King, Medgar Evers, Malcolm X, John Lennon. They all said 'Try to live together peacefully.' BAM! Right in the fuckin' head. Apparently, we're not ready for that."

-George Carlin

Whistleblowers, Tis, peace activists.

One of few, who stood up for many.

The true heroes of America have been killed by those who claim to protect us. The irony never stops, until we decide to stop it.

The only hope of the whistleblower is to see a change in the world. For killers to stop killing, for humanity to become humane. For men to start acting like men, and confronting people if they have a problem with them; for civilization to become civilized.

We are no longer in high school. We are no longer joining cliques, fraternities, and organizations to represent us as a man. Those who choose to remain in the Peter Pan stage of life, refusing to "grow up," shall be treated as such by us adults. Those who bully others to feel powerful are as the animal abusers who enjoy watching their pets live in pain.

Stalking is a mental illness. As ironic as is may seem, I wish the best for those who participate in COINTELPRO. I want to see them get better in the head. I don't want to watch a mental patient drown in their own vomit, and I don't want to watch a COINTELPRO participant create his own demise through stupidity and childishness.

However, as previously mentioned, I will have no compassion for those who rape others. Whether it is personal space, genetalia, or the simple act of stealing someone else's freewill by implementation of a senseless law that invades someone else's privacy or right to life — rape is rape.

If I were judge, no rapist would leave my courtroom with the ability to ever, ever, ever rape another human being. Whatever it takes, we have to stop the crime.

Same deal with Operation Phoenix, COINTELPRO, and Project Monarch.

I, as other peace activists, wish
nothing but the best for humanity. I love
life. What I hate, is to watch someone take
that ability from someone else. What I love
more than life, however, is to watch others
enjoy life.

That is not called "co-dependent." That
is called "compassion for my fellow man."

Someday, we will realize that we are
all brothers and sisters. When we grow up,
fighting as children is no longer an option.

*"The only way to make a slave stay a slave — is to
make him think that he is free.*

*When people believe that free-thinkers are insane,
they choose to remain a slave. A slave to the
system, a slave to delusion, a slave to ignorance
of reality by choice. After all, ignorance is
bliss — and truth is stranger than fiction."*

"Peace cannot be kept by force; it can only
be achieved by understanding."

- Albert Einstein

Footnotes:

1)

http://www.wired.com/dangerroom/2009/07/court-to-def
endant-stop-blasting-that-mans-mind/

2)

http://en.wikipedia.org/wiki/1953_Iranian_coup_d'%C3
%A9tat

3) http://www.youtube.com/watch?v=Ni2FFSAhTcA

4) http://www.wired.com/2010/10/fbi-tracking-device/

About the author

Michael D. Fleming
(1983-[hasn't croaked yet])
was born in Bristol,
Tennessee, to Native-American
(Cherokee) and German
descent, and grew up in
Johnson City, Tennessee.

Comments and corrections are always welcome. **Further readings by this author are available at:**

www.MichaelDavidFleming.com

This book is dedicated to the memory of Gus Grissom and Michael Ruppert. Where you are, there are no demons to torture you with COINTELPRO.

42693041R00042

Made in the USA
Middletown, DE
16 April 2019